Advance Praise for *Child Safety 101*

Parents—don't assume you know all there is to know on helping your child stay Safe! Even after thirty years of working with children and families, this book contains many practical and wise ideas that I never thought of on how to teach your child to have a "learned instinct" to avoid the dangers from increasingly savvy predators.

—Laurel Hines, L.C.S.W.,
Child and Family Therapist

Simply put, this is a must read for parents.

—Chuck Whitlock,
Award Winning Investigative Journalist

Caretakers of children, should it be parents, relatives or foster parents, need to be aware of the ways they can keep their children safe. This handbook gives very simple, detailed instructions on ways to protect your child while not creating a "world of monsters." If parents provided the necessary protection for children, there would be less need for government protective agencies.

—Sharon Gustafson, MSW
State of Oregon Child Welfare, Supervisor, Retired

CHILD SAFETY 101

101+ Safety Tips for Protecting Your Child

Also by Benny Mares

Executive Protection: A Professional's Guide to Bodyguarding

CHILD SAFETY 101

101+ Safety Tips for Protecting Your Child

by

Benny Mares

Retired Los Angeles Police Officer

Foreword by

Chuck Whitlock

Award Winning Investigative Correspondent and Author

Unlimited Publishing
Bloomington, Indiana

Contents

Dedication

For my loving and encouraging wife Kristie

and

our beautiful granddaughters,
Alexandra, Adrianna, and Isabella;

also

for the children of the world
who have a right to live in safety

and

the organizations who strive to make that right a reality.

Foreword

IF EVERY PARENT in America uses the lessons in Benny Mares's *Child Safety 101*, we could put child molesters out of business overnight. This is a down-to-earth, practical guide that could save your child's life.

I can remember at least three instances in my childhood when child molesters approached me. I think many adults can recall such a childhood experience. In my case, I didn't get into the stranger's car; I had the good sense to simply turn and run. Some children aren't as lucky. And, as we all know, being molested can have lifetime repercussions.

As a reporter, I've investigated these predators. They can be your child's uncle, your next door neighbor, or a soccer coach. Few, if any, are ever rehabilitated. One investigation I did for the national television show *Extra* required that I take the identity of a convicted pedophile and apply for jobs in New York. In one day, I was hired by a day care center and a parochial grammar school. Neither of them did a criminal background check prior to hiring me, which would have revealed that my assumed name and social security number belonged to a child molester.

In *Child Safety 101*, Benny provides sound advice to reduce your child's exposure to dangerous predators. As an example, he tells you not to put your children's names on their jacket or knapsacks because a child molester will know their names and use them when he approaches. *Child Safety 101* will help you improve the odds should your child encounter a pedophile. Simply put, it's a must-read for parents. The small price you paid for this book coupled with the short amount of time to read it will pay big dividends in terms of your peace of mind and your children's safety.

—Chuck Whitlock
Investigative Correspondent, Author and Speaker

Chuck Whitlock is a recipient of the **National Headliner Award** for Outstanding Investigative Reporting, the **Society of Professional Journalists' Sigma Chi Award** for Television Investigative Reporting, and an **Excellence in Consumer Education in Television Broadcasting Award** from the National Association on Consumer Agency Administrators.

Preface

FOR OVER TWENTY YEARS I lived by the motto "To Protect and To Serve" as a Los Angeles Police Officer. I carried that precept to the private sector into the world of executive protection. As a police officer, I responded to numerous child abuse calls, and reports involving predators of many types, strangers, friends, and even relatives. As a personal protection specialist, I was responsible, nationally and internationally, for the protection of business persons, celebrities, and foreign dignitaries. I've had the responsibility of providing protection for adults and children of all ages.

In writing *Child Safety 101*, I have drawn on my public and private sector experiences and compiled safety tips intended specifically for the protection of children. Unlike the reactive actions of a police officer responding to the scene of a crime already committed, this book addresses protecting the child in a proactive manner as a bodyguard would approach protecting his client. Safety tips and discussions are presented in an "inner-to-outer" perimeter approach, beginning in the home, moving to the neighborhood, discussing day care and school, and continuing to areas away from the children's center of comfort, their home. This is the coverage due to the unmistakable fact that a child is a potential victim in practically every area.

In the field of executive protection, not everyone can afford the services of a bodyguard. Many executives hire a personal protection agent to teach their personnel to protect themselves. The agent will instruct the employees on how to recognize potentially dangerous situations and how to develop the ability to play "what if" scenarios. This training will enable the individual to be mentally prepared and able to possibly avoid being targeted as a victim of crime.

As the corporate executive protects employees by teaching them safety awareness, a parent's responsibility is to the child. A child needs to be mentally prepared to distinguish and handle sensitive or dangerous predicaments. This parental obligation is met by a continuous child safety awareness education that has its origin in the home at an early age.

Child safety awareness programs have emerged in almost every community due to the growing concern of parents and teachers. Almost daily, the media features stories about child victims of abduction or sexual crimes. Only recently have parents refrained from saying "I never thought it could happen in this community," as it is widely accepted that sexual deviants and child predators target intended victims in every locale, neighborhood streets, schools, playgrounds, and even houses of worship.

Child Safety 101 is based on the premise that every parent is a concerned parent. A concerned parent is aware that there is a worldwide problem of missing, sexually abused, and murdered children. A concerned parent knows that this problem is not caused only by strangers. A concerned parent knows not to believe "It can't happen to my child." A concerned parent knows that child safety awareness is a major deterrent to criminal behavior. *Child Safety 101* addresses these issues in stressing child safety awareness.

May your child always be safe.

Introduction

THIS BOOK primarily addresses the issues that our children are confronted with in our society caused by pedophiles, sex offenders, and child molesters (redundancy at its lowest level). Individual chapters deal with our children's daily activities where these creatures may roam. As parents, we must grasp the safety concepts to educate our children so they may defend themselves against these predators.

The breath of fresh air into this cloud of gloom is that due to the vast amount of publicity of the fate of such beautiful souls as 6-year-old Adam Walsh, 12-year-old Amber Hagerman, 7-year-old Megan Kanka, and so many others, our society continues to force these criminals deeper into the shadows and simultaneously protects our children by stressing child safety education. All forms of media contribute to our children learning faster and being more attuned to our world, for better or worse. Child safety education contributes to protecting our children from the "worse."

The ultimate goal of child safety organizations is to provide sufficient information to educate all children to a level of being able to discourage any predator from considering them as their next victim.

Children from many generations grew up hearing cautionary advice being given to little girls, such as "be careful—don't talk to strangers," while little boys were sent along their way with such guidance as "be a good boy—come straight home." The general perception in our communities was predators targeted little girls, not little boys. The general notion was "strangers" were males and the idea of homosexual preying was unthinkable, or at least unspoken of. The singling out of only little girls is a misconception; boys and girls are targeted victims of child molesters worldwide. With our modern technology, a predator's tentacles have the ability to reach into almost every home, school, and library.

All children must be taught child safety in order to be mentally prepared to discourage child molesters from focusing on them as their intended victims.

Educating a child on child safety practices should not be perceived as difficult or threatening. Safety education begins at home, just as safety rules are taught to children as they grow and their ability to understand increases. When the question of when a parent should begin teaching child safety to their child is asked, the answer is: as "child safety" encompasses many areas, *all* areas can blend into one's educational procedures. Just as a child is taught at a toddler age, "no, no—that is hot," or "no—that's sharp—don't touch," very early in a child's life he or she can learn "no, no—don't open the door without Mommy." As situations arise, child safety rules may be taught.

Child safety can be taught in a variety of ways. A very effective and highly recommended method is role-playing using "what if" scenarios. Upon observing a child safety-related situation in the media, television, newspaper, magazines, etc., ask your child "what would you do if a person came up to you and . . . ?" This would present an opportunity to discuss other child safety rules. Look for every opportunity to discuss child safety with your child.

Child safety education

must have been the inspiration

of a loving parent.

1

Home

Crime prevention begins with safety education at home.
Safety education can be taught with an informal, systematic
approach to the subject. Children will not become frightened
when child safety issues are raised if they are normally discussed.
Hypotheticals are a practical approach to protective information.
Play the "what if" game whenever a child safety-related story
is featured in the media. Safety habits and cautious behavior
are the results of regular child safety discussions.

**Teach your child his or her name, address, and telephone
number at an early age.**
When small children become lost or separated from their parents,
the ability to inform adults of their full names, addresses, and
telephone numbers accelerates the process of reuniting them
with their parents. In addition to the knowledge of their own
information, knowledge of their parents' full names would be
extremely helpful to anyone assisting them.

**Teach your child to use a peephole or window to identify
anyone at the door before opening the door.**
Even if you are home, this is a recommended practice; however,
it is critical for children to follow this rule if they are home
alone. If your child does not recognize the person at the door,
your child should not open it, even if the person appears to
be a respectable figure of society such as a postal worker or

police officer. There should be no harm in children advising people that they cannot open the door and that a parent cannot come to the door. A genuine person of authority will respect the fact that a child follows such safety rules. In the event the person at the door persists in trying to convince your child to open the door, let your child know it would be proper to call 911 for help. A police officer would not hesitate to assist a frightened child. Note: it would not be wise for the child to ignore the person at the door by remaining quiet. Many burglars "case" neighborhoods to determine an easy target because no one is home. Such a person would leave rather than chance having the police summoned.

A child should never tell an unknown telephone caller "no one is home."

There are many methods to obtain someone's telephone number. Several professions regularly use a "reverse directory" which allows the person to see a telephone number as it is listed with an address, or an address and then the telephone number. These directories provide telephone numbers either by residential blocks or in numerical order. A child telling a caller that no one is home informs the caller that the child is home alone. Have your child respond to any telephone inquiries for you by saying that you are "busy right now," or give them other specific instructions on what to say if you are not home.

Educate children about telephone surveys and tell them not to answer any questions.

A telephone survey is a method many callers use to obtain important personal information about individuals and families. Although the caller, male or female, may sound very nice and friendly, advise your child to never give personal information to anyone on the telephone.

Keep a list of emergency numbers near the telephone.

Situations of an emergency nature may arise at any time, or may merely be in a child's imagination. A list conveniently placed near the telephone could avert a potential crisis. At the very least, a child's ability to contact a loved one for comforting advice at a stressful time silently implies that you are there for your child at all times.

Small children should be taught to call 911 in an emergency, and told what an emergency would be. The media continually features stories of young heroes who called 911 when faced with an emergency. Prepare your child on how to react if confronted with an emergency.

Avoid giving children clothing or items with their names on them.

Knowledge of a person's name is generally an advantage. A person addressed by his or her first name is very likely to respond in a friendly manner when approached. This is especially true of a young child. Any name tag identifies the child and gives an advantage to a stranger. Items to avoid identifying include clothing, backpacks, lunch boxes, and jewelry, to name a few. Gift shops are saturated with personalized jewelry for small children. Such items allow someone to compliment the item of jewelry, "That is a real nice bracelet (necklace, ring, etc.)" while observing the child's name. Avoid items that give personal information about a child to everyone within eyesight of the child.

Make sure your child's room is not easily accessible from the outside of the home.

Ground level rooms are accessible from the outside of the home; however, efforts must be made to prevent or deter someone from entering your child's bedroom from the outside. Precautions can be taken to discourage an intruder, such as ensuring that a window is limited in the available space needed for ventilation, or ensuring that there is a dead-bolt lock on any outside door. Each evening, routinely check that all windows and doors are locked.

Teach your child a "code" word.

A code word is a special word or phrase created for identification purposes between you and your child. Airlines use this technique for identification of someone designated to pick up a child traveling alone. Airline personnel meet the person picking up the child and ask for the "code" word, knowing the parent gave the "word" to this designated person. This practice can be used anywhere your child needs to be picked up by anyone other than a parent.

Your children should know that only in an emergency situation would someone other than you or a regular guardian pick them up from school, call them with any requests, or show up asking them to do something on your directions. In such a situation, inform your child that the person would know the "code" word. Stress with your child that this word or phrase is for emergency situations only and not to be told to anyone. Practice "what-if" scenarios that would involve using this practice.

If a person approaching your child has no knowledge of a "code" word or attempts to mislead the child when your child asks about a "code" word, your child should get away from that person immediately.

Teach your children not to approach your home if the doors are open, a window is broken, or they see signs of a break-in.

This is a family rule. Avoid entering your residence if there are visible signs of criminal activity outside the home. Telephone the police and have them respond to investigate. Advise your child to seek help from a neighbor who can call the police. It would never be advisable to confront an intruder.

References and background checks on all household employees are essential.

Do a thorough background check on any domestic help who will have access to your home or property on a regular basis. This includes housekeepers, gardeners, handymen, and everyone who would be familiar with your schedules and especially your child. Ask for references and make it a point to check with all previous employers.

Many crimes, including those against children, have been committed by trusted household employees.

Encourage your child to approach you with any of their concerns.

Every child should be advised that he or she can feel comfortable discussing anything with parents. Children avoid discussing sensitive issues with their parents because they feel embarrassed or they feel they will not be believed by their parents. A child who feels loved and trusted will not hesitate to approach a parent with concerns. Many child safety tips throughout this book will be encompassed by this rule, such as your child being told to keep a secret, an adult wrongfully approaching your child, and a child's personal concerns.

A parent's natural instinct is to protect a child.

Teach children safety and you develop

their instincts to protect themselves.

Babysitters

References and background checks on babysitters are essential.

Just as references and background checks are critical for employees of a day care center, it is critical that a babysitter be thoroughly checked prior to employment. A babysitter will be coming into the privacy of your home. She or he will be completely responsible for the safety of your child. At a minimum, check references even for the neighborhood teenager or young adult. Your inquiries should focus on the babysitter's reputation, associates, and current social responsibilities. You can never be too cautious when checking babysitter references.

Make sure your babysitter has all your emergency numbers.

It is critical that a babysitter be provided with your emergency telephone numbers, even more so than a teacher or day care provider. A babysitter is alone in your home and in the case of an emergency must have all means of contacting you immediately.

Provide strict instructions to your babysitter for emergency situations.

In an emergency or crisis situation, panic is a normal reaction. Informative, reviewed procedures dealing with these situations have proven to reduce panic. Provide and review strict emergency instructions with your babysitter. Even inexperienced young adults will react favorably to a crisis if they are mentally prepared. Inform your babysitter of the procedures and put a written copy of the instructions in a location readily available to the babysitter, such as on the refrigerator or near the telephone.

Restrict your babysitter from social phone calls.

A babysitter's primary responsibility is for the safety and well being of your child. Social phone calls divert a babysitter's attention from her (or his) duties. Any parent can attest to the fact that it only takes a small diversion to allow children to hurt themselves. Telephone activity should be kept to a minimum (necessary conversations only).

Set rules for your babysitter regarding friends visiting.

If you allow your babysitter to have a friend visit or accompany her/him to watch your child, know the individual coming over. The majority of young adults are very responsible and can be trusted, but be aware that many child abuse cases or molestations have occurred by a babysitter's boyfriend or lover. Babysitting is a trusted responsibility and the individual's complete attention should be focused on your child. It is recommended the babysitter sits alone.

May the safety of your child

always be your first concern.

Neighborhood

A child should always play with a friend.

The "Buddy System" is safer than playing alone. There is so much truth in the saying "There's safety in numbers." Statistics show that child molesters typically prey on the lone child. Encourage your child that always playing with a buddy allows each child to watch out for the other. This practice also discourages pedophiles from watching one child at play. A small child may be alarmed when learning this rule, so it is suggested you explain to your child that always playing with someone allows the other child to call you if your child is hurt. As the child grows, the rationale for the "buddy system" can be fully explained.

Know your child's friends and their addresses and telephone numbers.

There have been numerous accounts of children being reported missing and neighbors and police officers searching for hours before the child was discovered playing in a friend's home nearby. In the event of a child being reported missing, police officers would welcome all leads, such as names, addresses, and telephone numbers of your child's friends. Many times, such information would have expedited locating a child. Maintain a file of this and other pertinent information on your child and have it readily available should your child become missing or unusually late. This information would allow you to begin a thorough search of all your child's contacts. In the chapter on documentation, the importance of knowing your child's friends and all related information is stressed further.

An additional rule in this area is: Meet your child's new friends. When your child meets new friends, listen to your child as they tell you of the friend and plan to meet the child as soon as you can. This will allow you to know the child and have additional information for your child's identification packet.

A child should never play in buildings, cars, or places where they could be locked in.

Explain to your child the dangers of playing in areas they could be trapped inside. Highlight the fact that cars, trunks, abandoned refrigerators, to name a few examples, could rise in heat and suffocate a child. Know that predators are also aware of such areas. Children will generally run for help if a friend is trapped, thereby leaving a child alone and vulnerable for the briefest of moments. In a very short period of time a child could suffocate or a child predator could act.

Always go with your children when they go door-to-door.

The most notable activity where children go door-to-door is Halloween for trick-or- treating. This fun-filled day generally encompasses parents going with their child door-to-door showing their child's costumes and observing the expectant dwellers giving treats. Other activities such as fundraisers, school projects, or paper sales requiring a child to go door-to-door should be supervised by an accompanying parent or adult. In these latter scenarios the home occupants are not expecting a child to knock on their door, and therefore are surprised to see a child standing alone.

Many defendants, during their child molestation trials, have pled that their acts were not planned, but were simply acts of opportunity. Although an individual may have a predisposition to molest a child, he or she may not act upon their thoughts until the "right opportunity" presents itself. The lone child at the door may be perceived as "opportunity knocking." Children soliciting anything door-to-door should be accompanied by an adult.

Establish "Safe Homes" in your neighborhood.

This is an extension of the neighborhood watch concept. A safe home is a home where a child can go in an emergency situation and feel safe. This practice has a positive ripple effect in the community. It establishes and builds friendship and community ties among the neighbors, alerts everyone entering the area that it is a caring neighborhood, and gives comfort to children, knowing that their families and neighbors care for their safety.

A branch of the safe home plan is the telephone tree. A telephone tree is a plan of action where neighbors exchange their telephone numbers and know, if they are notified of an emergency, their designated action is to call another concerned neighbor on the list, the next neighbor calls another, and so on until everyone has been notified. It is a recommended practice that each neighbor calls two others, causing an overlapping of contacts and making every effort to ensure no one has been overlooked. In the event of an emergency, such as a lost child, one phone call to a neighbor sets in motion many calls, until everyone is alerted of the situation and is acting upon the call.

Have your child practice ways of alerting others if he or she is being forced into a vehicle or building.

Noise in any situation draws the attention of even the most apathetic observer. A screaming child's voice is so piercing an attacker would be completely foolish in continuing their abduction efforts. Bystanders would most likely take some action to assist a child. Many people would take overt action against the attacker, while others would passively call for help or record a license number or description of the attacker. All assistance would contribute to the attacker moving on and hopefully being apprehended. Inform your child to kick, scream, throw items, and run to a safe, public place. The more discussion and practice of this type of situation the more an instinctive reaction is developed within the child to ward off attackers.

Never let a child walk to or wait alone at a bus stop.

It is well known that child molesters stalk children. Predators also watch for the child walking alone or waiting alone for transportation, feeling the children will be vulnerable to deceptive ploys. Child molesters will offer children rides after telling them the bus has broken down or will be extremely late due to some school emergency, and will entice the child to accept a ride in their vehicle. Children are more susceptible to such fabrications and lures in inclement weather, dreading the task of walking in the rain or snow. Generally, a bus stop where numerous children wait together is safe, but even a single parent waiting with the children serves as a deterrent and increases the perimeter of safety.

Shortcuts through dark and unsupervised areas should not be taken by children.

This rule speaks for itself of the potential dangers of seedy characters lurking in the dark, ready to pounce on unsuspecting victims, children being the most vulnerable. Children need to be reminded of areas that should be avoided in their routes. Continually include this rule in your safety education discussions.

Use the public files to check for registered sex offenders.
Know your neighbors. Information that was previously confidential is now available under the Public Information Act, and Megan's Law provides access to sex offender information. The teenage boy next door, the new neighbor on the corner, or the lonely man down the block, may have a background you need to be aware of. Registered sex offender information will inform you of such individual's addresses in your city (see Megan's Law in chapter on Notable Laws and Alerts).

The safety of a child

should be everyone's concern.

Day Care

Know your day care provider well.

A reputable day care center is fully licensed and accredited. A licensing agency generally conducts a background investigation on the day care staff. The key word here is *generally*. It is imperative that you personally inquire about the backgrounds, qualifications, and references of any center you intend to entrust with your child's welfare. This is especially necessary if the day care provider is a "friend-of-a-friend" who is less expensive and more convenient.

Keep your day care provider information up-to-date.

Advise your day care provider that you want to be informed when additional staff is employed, and that you want to have their credentials or background checks verified. A 19 year-old male was recently convicted and sentenced to prison for molesting three little girls, ages 3, 4, and 5 at the day care center where he worked as a teacher's aide. This was a summer position for the sex offender. You have a right to current information on any facility staff member caring for your child.

Insist on parental control with your day care service.

You should have unlimited access to all areas of a day care center. You should not be expected to provide prior notification that you are checking on, visiting or picking up your child. If the center prohibits unscheduled visits by you, find another day care service. Many scandals, warranted and unwarranted, have plagued the day care industry; therefore, it would be highly unusual for a facility to have an unscheduled visitation rule. Remember, it is your child. The day care center staff work for you. You have complete authority in all matters dealing with your child.

Provide your day care provider with all your emergency numbers.

The same as with your babysitter and school, a day care provider must have all methods of contacting you in the event of an emergency. If, due to your busy schedule, attempts to reach you may result in contacting your voice mail, also provide your provider with the numbers of friends and relatives. Criminal attempts have been made to pick up a child by using a ruse, claiming their parent is unavailable due to an accident or some other emergency. Under such circumstances, most day care providers would know to call the authorities before releasing a child, but should also immediately contact the child's parent.

Advise your day care provider of any change in plans.

Your provider must be personally notified by you if you have given someone else permission to pick up your child, even if that person has picked up your child before. Information should be given to the day care personnel as to who may be allowed to pick up your child, so the provider is familiar with the expected person after your notification of the change in plans. Additionally, if there is a change in any information, such as a custody ruling, immediately notify your provider of who is *not* allowed to pick up your child.

Communicate with your child.

Make it a regular practice to discuss your child's daily activities with them. Was it a fun day? Did they enjoy the care center people? What did they do? Observing your child's reactions can also answer your questions as well as their direct answers. Look for signs of irritation, sadness, embarrassment, or denial. Failure to discuss daily activities on a regular basis may cause a child to accept improper behavior as a normal act by someone of authority (also review the rule regarding "secrets").

A parent's enthusiasm to teach

encourages a child to learn.

5

School

Know your child's school schedule.
Knowledge of your child's schedule as well as their after-school activities is critical. Merely knowing where your child is at all times is crucial, and is important should you need to make immediate contact.

"Back-to-school" is a time to stress "to-and-from" school safety.
Education encompasses a wide variety of subjects generally associated with school. "To-and-From" school safety discussions should be generated at home. Discuss with your children the potential hazards of diverting from their school routes, failure to keep you informed of their activities, or taking advice from others who might lead them astray. Use hypotheticals to discuss this area of safety with your child on a regular basis.

The quickest route to school may not be the safest route.
Know all the routes your child may take to and from the school. This rule supports the "to-and-from" safety discussion. Knowledge of every possible route available to your child will expand the area of your safety discussions and will enhance your search area should you need to look for your child or assist others. Share with your child the necessity of having this route information and openly discuss emergency planning

tactics such as areas you would initially search if they were extremely late coming home.

Teach your child to come directly home from school.

Your child will appreciate your love and concern in you having the satisfaction of knowing they are safe at home after school. Establish a procedure for notifying you that they have arrived safely from school. Notification takes a very short period of time as compared to the stress and anxiety in realizing later that your child failed to arrive home and they must be located. If your child wants to go somewhere with their friends after school, make it a rule that they must call for your permission before they leave the school.

Grade school children should know their teacher's name and their school's name.

Even with the tightest of security, small children have an uncanny ability to wander away from designated areas. Should a child stray from a playground or school classroom and be noticed by an adult, knowledge of his or her teacher's name and/or school's name will greatly assist in a safe return to the school.

Know your child's friends at school.

Your child may have friends you are unaware of because they live in a different part of the city. Discuss this possibility with your child and have a list of names, addresses, and telephone numbers of these friends. Make arrangements to meet these school friends socially away from the school environment. This is relevant information if your child is late from school, but also necessary for you to determine the type of child your child feels comfortable with and your child's likes and dislikes.

Your child's teachers should have every method of contacting you.

There are numerous unexpected situations that arise with children that necessitate contact with their parents prior to other officials being able to take any action. A teacher having the role of a surrogate parent can take certain actions, however the law mandates parental consent in most medical emergencies. School procedures generally require parental notification involving any safety issue. Any parent would insist on nothing less, therefore a teacher or school should be provided with every number to contact you.

Your child should tell you and their teacher if there is a school bully.

An older or "tough" kid at your child's school may threaten another child with bodily harm in an attempt to intimidate the child into giving them something or doing something for them. A child of this nature needs to be reported.

Advise your child that a "code of silence" surrounding school violence endangers everyone. Reporting a child who is older or unfamiliar to your child (or his or her classmates) is extremely important, as this "bully" may be from another area and is preying on the younger children attempting to find a submissive victim.

A rule that dovetails into this advice is that your children should also feel comfortable discussing any incident with you where they feel picked-on, harassed or teased at school. Many children fail to discuss such problems with their parents or school officials because of fear of retaliation. Make sure the child in question, the bully, is confronted with their actions anonymously, rather than as a direct result of a child reporting them. A recommended approach would be for the school official would be "It's come to our attention that you have been asking other children for money . . ." rather than "Billy says you have been rough with him." If sexual activity is involved, immediately contact the police. This type of activity demands official action and investigation as to whether there are other victims of this offender.

A child's ability to learn is

directly proportionate to a parent's

desire to teach.

Public Places

Keep your child with you while grocery shopping.

There are so many items of interest in a grocery store, and with today's stores larger and offering much more than food, a child's space is limited only to his or her imagination. Naturally, the ideal situation is to always have your child with you; however, in the event your child wanders away, teach him or her to wait for you by the cashier.

Many stores have implemented a "Code-Adam", named for 6 year-old Adam Walsh who was separated from his mother in a store, abducted and brutally murdered. "Code-Adam" is broadcast throughout the store, putting every employee on alert that there is a child missing in the store and they should attempt to locate the child. In any case, notify a store employee if you are separated from your child while shopping. If the store does not have a missing child code, the employee would have similar means to notify other employees and all shoppers. Collectively everyone could assist in finding your child, possibly standing with a cashier, as advised by you.

Take your child with you if you need to use the restroom while at a restaurant.

Never leave a small child alone. The potential dangers are so apparent for a child being left alone. A child could wander away, be abducted, or suffer a medical emergency. No matter how familiar you are with a location or its personnel, never leave a small child alone. A like rule in this context is: when your children need to use a restaurant's restroom, go with them. Many child molestations have occurred in public restrooms. Imagine all areas to which this rule would be applicable: theaters, hotels, airports, any public restroom. Constantly supervise younger children in any public area. Keep them within arm's reach, your "public safety zone."

Avoid being separated in a crowded shopping mall by holding your child's hand.

Small children's curiosity causes them to wander. This can be prevented by holding your child's hand. Shopping malls are extremely crowded, especially during peak seasons such as the holidays. Busy shoppers, in a rush, like to "bob and weave" in and out of shoppers. For the most part, these rapidly moving shoppers separate husbands and wives, sisters, friends, and parents from their children unintentionally. However, in a very brief moment, an intentional separation can result in a child abduction. Keep your child close, allowing no threatening gap between you.

Prearrange a time and place to meet after shopping with older children.

Older children can be given a "window of time," 10-15 minutes for example, to meet at a predetermined location. Have them meet you and obtain your permission if they wish to continue in the mall or get transportation from someone else. However, for security purposes, all parties should coordinate plans.

Teach your child to advise an adult if they become separated from you in a mall, but that they should not go anywhere with the adult.

This rule supports the teaching that a child should remain by the cashier if lost. A child should know they can approach an adult to help them locate you, but they are to remain at one location, not walk with the adult anywhere. An additional theory is to teach your child to always stay where they last saw you if they get separated from you. Whatever rule both parent and child abide by will contribute to a happy reunion.

As children's understanding increases, teach them the difference between them approaching a "stranger" for assistance and a "strange" adult approaching them for assistance (see the chapter on strangers for complete analysis).

Keep your children in sight and supervise their activities on a playground.

Although there are many parents observing children at play on a public playground, no one has the personal interest you show your own children. Be aware of their activities and be near enough so others know your child is being supervised. A public playground is a haven for child predators. Some predators pose as a single parent watching children at play. They may say they don't have custody of their child that day, but still enjoy watching other children. Staying close to your child deters anyone with intentions of approaching your child.

If your child wanders away in a park or a playground, teach him or her to approach another family to help find you.

With all your good intentions of supervision, a child may still be able to wander away. In an amusement park, on a playground or at a public gathering, a child may stray off and get lost. Teach your child that another family with children is safe and will help locate you. As soon as you lose sight of your child, notify someone with authority at the event. This person would be in a position to notify security and alert others of your child's description. Most likely, the other family would also request someone to call security.

On amusement park rides, always have your small children completely in sight.

The majority of rides for small children have the entrance and exits closely situated. This may be the favorable position to observe your child's ride. This would be the preferred area to greet your child upon their exit, but most importantly, position yourself to watch your child get off the ride and as they walk to the exit. A small child can easily be lifted over a barricade in the "blink of an eye". Anyone with such an intent will be observing children who are not being closely supervised.

If you are not in sight, teach your child to remain in a designated area after getting off a ride.

If your children get off an amusement park ride and do not see you immediately, teach them to remain where they got off the ride, at the exit area. They should ask the attendant for assistance, but they are not to go away from the ride with the attendant, or wander away by themselves in search of you.

As the glitter of theme parks have a tendency to lure children to the various rides and attractions, a child's attention would be distracted, which could complicate locating your child. Remaining at the exit area of a ride would comfort your child, knowing that's where you were last seen and would soon return. A wandering child signals to many that the child is alone and vulnerable.

Always put small children in first on amusement park trams.

For the majority of parents this will be a "Really?" rule, as tram transportation doors all close collectively—how could it be possible for a parent to neglect to assist a small child? The rationale for this advice was observed first-hand. On a Disneyworld Magic Kingdom tram, the very alert attendants noticed a two-year old girl was left behind as the tram rapidly moved forward to its next destination. At the following stop the assisting attendant reunited the child with her parents and two other young siblings. The little girl was the youngest of the family. The father questioned, "Honey, why didn't you get on?" The mother stated she noticed the daughter missing after the tram began moving. Should you ever get separated from your child, notify an attendant immediately for their assistance.

When you are camping, tell your child never to leave the campsite area without your permission.

Campgrounds and natural parks provide enormous amounts of natural beauty, panoramic views, rivers and streams, and many exciting areas that may lure a young inquisitive child from your campsite. A child may also be enticed by a stranger inviting the child to see "a live teddy bear" or a baby deer. Discuss similar scenarios with your child while emphasizing your rule to not go anywhere without your permission.

Advise your child if they ever get lost in a camping area to approach a parent in a nearby campsite for help.

If a child wanders away from a campsite, it is easy to get disoriented and turned around. If other campsites are nearby, teach your child to seek help from an adult. In the event other sites are relatively far for a young child, advise your child to remain in one location if they get lost and help will come to them. As with any search, if everyone including the person being sought is continually moving, locating the lost person becomes much more difficult.

Always keep your child in view at the beach.

Relax and enjoy the sun and the beach, but always keep your child in sight and within close proximity of your place in the sun. The beach is another location that can get very crowded.

A child can get distracted very easily. In the bright sunlight your vision can be momentarily blocked. It takes but a second for a child to wander into the water, be abducted, or get lost in the crowd.

A safe child is a happy child,

a happy child is a loving child,

a loving child becomes a loving parent, and

a loving parent teaches children child safety.

7

Hotels and Apartments

A building's laundry room is not a play area.

Don't allow your children to use a laundry room as a play area or meeting room. A laundry room is generally a warm, quiet, secluded area in a building where noise will not affect the residents. Transients or homeless individuals view this type of an area as a comfortable, convenient space to seek shelter. The criminal element of our society views these areas as perfect locations to prey on victims. Advise your children of the potential dangers of such areas, and that they should be accompanied by a parent when going to a building's laundry room.

Do not allow your child to play on the roof or in the basement of a building.

A basement, like a laundry room, presents many latent opportunities for the criminal mind. A basement of a building is generally a sound-suppressed area, sounds being muffled by the pipes, general construction, and various storage items. A warped individual seeking warm shelter, then observing children at play, may consider the scenario as an opportunity to sexually abuse a child. Keeping children out of dark hideaways may keep them out of harm's way.

A rooftop is similar in potential areas of concealment and presents the additional danger of extreme height. Both the basement and the roof are areas to avoid as children's play areas.

Do not rely completely on a hotel's security for your child's safety.

A hotel security force goes to great effort and expense to provide security for its guests, but it is limited in its abilities. Personnel, cameras, and procedures deter the majority of open criminal activity on hotel premises. As in other locations, many crimes go undetected. As a parent, you must protect your child from the ill intentions of others passing through the hotel. Keep in mind that everyone at the hotel is a stranger, good or bad, and many criminals commit their crimes while traveling, away from their familiar surroundings. Contribute to the safety efforts of the hotel by guarding your child against any person who could be viewing your child as a sexual object.

Children should use the hotel elevators, not the stairwells.

Many hotel guests allow their children to go to and from the hotel pool area unaccompanied. With this in mind, it is a good rule to never allow your child to use or play in the facility's stairwell. Instruct your child to use the hotel elevator at all times. A stairwell is too quiet and confining. It presents numerous hazards to young and unsuspecting children. A child could fall, become injured, and be outside the hearing of anyone who could render assistance. Stairwells have also been the sites of rapes, molestations, and many other crimes. The preferred practice would be to escort younger children throughout any public area.

Escort your child as they explore the facilities of a hotel.

A hotel is filled with many trap doors, the numerous rooms on every floor. Laundry, maintenance, and other guest rooms pose a potential threat of providing a place to hide or assault a child. A child walking alone through the halls of a hotel would be looked upon as an easy target by a predator. Child molesters develop highly effective methods of luring children into compromising situations, while other sex offenders are satisfied merely to grab a child, assault the child, and flee from the hotel. Even on a short trip from the room, such as to a vending machine or to get ice at the end of the hall, escorting your child is a safety precaution worth the effort.

Supervise your child in the hotel swimming pool.

Swimming pools attract sexual predators because they can openly observe children at play wearing only bathing suits. The more crowded the pool the more comfortable the pedophile.

As you supervise your child, watch for the lone adult, or older child, swimming near the children. Sex offenders have been known to swim near groups of children and "brush" a child's private areas as they pass. The unsuspecting child never realizes they have been assaulted as they continue to play in the water. If a child reports they have been touched, the offender profusely apologizes for the "misunderstanding" and they are prepared to explain their pool exercise that may have been too close to the children. Watch also for the older child who continually tickles small children in the pool, as this is a method of covertly groping a child.

Never let your guard down in a hotel room.

A hotel has a relaxing atmosphere, especially when checking in. Vacation is, and should be, an enjoyable time, but don't let your child safety guard down, because others may be watching for signs of mental relaxation and safety weakness. Home safety rules are equally applicable for a hotel room: children should not answer the door; don't give information to anyone on the telephone, etc. (review the home safety section). A good rule for your "home away from home" is to have your child safety concerns with you at all times, or even at a more heightened awareness level, since you arc in a new environment.

Educate a child in safety

and help create a safer world.

Strangers

Not every "stranger" is a stranger.

Everyone unfamiliar to us is a stranger, but not every stranger is bad or untrustworthy. There has been such a negative connotation to the term "stranger" that many child safety organizations prefer term "trusted" and "untrusted adult". Here it is important to note that many crimes, including child molestation, rapes, and abductions are committed by not a "stranger" or "untrusted adult", but unfortunately by a family member or someone known and trusted by the victim. The fact that a pedophile can be familiar or unfamiliar to us emphasizes the need for child safety education. (For the purposes of this chapter, the terms "stranger" and "untrusted adult" will be synonymous, and "trusted adult" will be self-explanatory.)

With respect to who is a stranger, educating your child may initially be confusing. Generally, a child will begin to sense who fits the category of a stranger who poses a threat, as they develop their own instincts after learning basic child safety rules. Initially a child may feel anxious when discussing threatening scenarios, self-protection, and standing up to verbally or physically warding off an adult. However, this anxiety will decrease as their level of confidence increases when they realize you will support their actions as they follow their safety rules.

Know your trusted adult.

Insist on references. Adults in positions of authority have been convicted as child molesters throughout the world. Many exposed predators move on, assume new identities, and seek employment or volunteer for positions where their responsibilities involve supervising children.

With the spotlight on abused and molested children in today's society, a respected coach or counselor will not be offended if asked for references. In fact, a true, caring professional working with children would be embarrassed by the adverse publicity affecting their chosen field, and would agree with a parent's concern for the safety and welfare of a child. Such vigilance by a parent is meant to flush out the unprofessional, the nemesis of respected guardians of children.

A child should stay beyond arm's length of a person they do not know.

Your child's warning signals should activate if they are approached by a stranger for assistance or directions. They should back away from the stranger. Generally, an adult requiring assistance of any kind or directions will approach another adult, not a child. Staying at least beyond arm's length allows children extra distance to begin running if a stranger attempts to touch or grab them. Under no circumstances should your child go near a vehicle slowing down when the driver calls the child over to it. Under this scenario, it would be advisable for your child to walk away quickly in the opposite direction. If your child feels threatened or scared, they should go to a public place, such as a store, and report the driver's action.

It is acceptable for a child to say "NO!" to an adult.

If your child is uncomfortable with the actions of an adult, tell him or her there is nothing wrong with telling the adult

"NO!" no matter who the adult is. A child can know to respect adults, but they must also know to respect themselves. If the older person makes them feel scared or uncomfortable they have the right to say "NO!" and move away from that adult. Teach your child that they have a right of choice. No one has a right to make your child do anything they do not want to do. Just say no!

Discuss examples of inappropriate behavior and touching. Discuss with your child when they should say "NO!"

If a stranger asks your child personal questions they should get away immediately.

An adult may ask a child friendly questions such as, "What's your name?" or "How old are you?" when the child is in the presence of a parent, however these are inappropriate questions if the child is alone. Unless the child is in need of assistance, an adult should not ask personal questions of a child. Personal questions and conversations lead to familiarity, and subsequently the person is no longer a "stranger" in the child's mind. Teach your child not to answer questions about themselves and to immediately get away from that individual.

Your children should always trust their feelings about what is right and what they should do.

Tell your children to pay attention to their own instincts. If it "just doesn't feel right," don't do it. If they feel you would not approve, don't do it. If they feel uncomfortable with what is taking place, don't do it. Tell them to listen to these inner feelings and they will know what is right and what they should do in most situations.

Your child may approach a stranger for help.

Instruct your child that if they are lost or need help it is okay to approach someone they do not know, the stranger, the trusted adult. The difference your child should be aware of is, when a child needs assistance, a stranger can be approached, but if a stranger approaches a child for assistance the child should be careful.

If a stranger wants to take your child's picture, your child should say "NO!"

An unfamiliar person may approach your child and ask them to pose for a picture. The person may say your child is very photogenic and could be a model. The individual may tell your child they are cute and would like them to pose with a small animal or stuffed toy. Explain such hypothetical situations with your child and teach them to always say no to such a person, and to get away immediately. As soon as possible your child should inform you of this person, and they should be reported. Most people with wrongful intentions will randomly take pictures of children, but some have been bold enough to request a pose. This would be an initial step to familiarity with the child and should send immediate signals to your child to move away. Many children have been abducted, some even murdered, by pedophiles posing as photographers.

If your child sees an unfamiliar adult taking pictures of children at play, have your child report this person.

Playgrounds and public parks are popular places for predators to watch children. There are even publications for and exchanged by pedophiles informing each other of the parks and playgrounds frequented by children in every major city. The first amendment freedom of speech prohibits closing down such publications.

Children should never approach the person taking the photographs, but merely observe and report their actions to a teacher or an adult they know. They should tell you about this person as soon as they see you. The person's actions may be innocent or they may be stalking children. It is best to let the authorities investigate and determine the person's intentions.

If a stranger asks your child to help find a lost animal, your child should say no and get away from that person.

Child safety experts have conducted parent-supervised tests using the "lost puppy" or "lost kitten" technique to lure small children who have been taught to never go with a stranger. This approach was very successful, to the amazement of the parents watching their child go with the "stranger." Role-play this approach extensively, especially with a susceptible young child, and stress the need to move away from anyone approaching him or her with such a request for assistance. This is a favorite ploy of child predators.

If someone grabs your child, teach them to scream, break loose, and run for help.

Teach your child that no one is allowed to grab them, and especially someone they do not know. If they are grabbed they should scream as loud as they can. As stated before, the piercing sound of a child's scream will not only attract attention, but should for an instance divert the attacker's concentration, allowing your child to break free and run.

Tell your child to run and scream until they are in a safe place and can receive help. They should report as much detail as they can remember about the attacker.

Teach your child "Never get into a car with someone you do not know."

This is an absolute rule your child must always follow. Under no circumstances should a child get into a vehicle with someone they do not know. Even if your child knows the person in the car, they should refuse to take a ride without your permission. For older children, this will become the "never hitchhike" rule.

If someone tells your child that you have been involved in an accident and he (or she) has been instructed to pick up your child, whether in a vehicle or on foot, tell your child they must refuse to go with the person, and have your child check immediately with a trusted adult. This, like the lost puppy ruse, is a common tactic of child abductors.

Teach older children "Never hitchhike or pick up strangers."
Older children should realize that in both cases an unknown journey is faced. This is a perfect example of someone being in control of his or her own destiny. These rules can be taught to children as hitchhikers are observed and as they are passed by. Whether or not the person standing in the roadway is a "good or bad stranger" would not be discovered until the stranger was met up close in a very confined area. A child growing up knowing never to get into a vehicle with someone unknown to them will support these rules.

Plant a safety seed

and help a child grow in safety.

Internet

Advise your children of the dangers of cyberspace.

The Internet is both elementary and complex, depending primarily upon one's generation. Children are now nurtured on computer activity and the Internet as baby boomers were weaned on pencil and paper while highlighting encyclopedias for study.

Cyberspace is the virtual space created by computer systems, also known as the information highway and the Internet. Children are limited only by their imaginations as they travel on this highway, but each child should also know the dangers on this well-traveled road. Many websites are for sexual exploitation, explicit images are sent through e-mail, and sex offenders target chat room participants. Chat rooms pose the most danger to children as these child predators attempt to entice communication, hoping it will escalate into physical contact. In this age of cyberspace activity, general child safety discussions should include the Internet.

Set rules for using the computer.

General rules should be set for using the computer, such as the time allowed to be online, the hours the computer is to be used, which sites are prohibited, and who is allowed to use the computer. Visitors should not be allowed access to your computer without supervision. It is advisable to spend computer time with your child where you can get involved in their interests and share quality computer time. The recommended location for the computer is the family room. This ensures parental supervision on all computer activity.

Set rules for Internet activity

Children using the Internet need parental supervision as much as in any other aspect of their lives. The Internet allows unlimited worlds to explore, and just as parents are responsible for guiding the inquisitive minds of their children as they grow into young adults, such guidance is required with Internet activity. In an effort to assist parents with enforcing rules and regulations, nearly all online and Internet Service Providers offer controls or blocking options. These services block or prohibit access to designated sites on the Internet.

Teach your child to never give personal information to anyone in cyberspace.

Personal information can be misused in many ways. Instruct your child to never give such information to anyone on the Internet. Chat rooms are abused by many adults posing as children and through this communication these adults attempt to draw out personal information from a child. This information may be an to attempt to arrange a personal meeting, find a child's home, or use such information for dangerous or illegal purposes. As an added protection for the Internet, note that most online service providers have software that will restrict outgoing personal information such as name, address, and telephone numbers from being sent online.

A screen name should not reveal personal information.

Your child should not use anything personal, such as their name or age when using a screen name. Predators utilizing the Internet chat rooms often select their intended victims by their screen names, for example "Suzy16." The Federal Bureau of Investigation has special agents who track this type of activity. Many arrests have been made where pedophiles have deceived children in chat rooms and have arranged or attempted to arrange face-to-face meetings.

Teach your child that people on the Internet may not be who they say they are.

Child predators can be very devious, knowing children are quite susceptible to ideas they have a strong interest in. These adults or older children tend to be Internet chameleons, able to change their personalities to blend with any child's interests and inquiries. People may even e-mail a "picture of themselves" to further the introduction online. Be aware, in such deceptions false photos will accompany the false information. The FBI warns that computer-based sex offenders may be of any age or sex.

Have your child inform you if an Internet contact wants to meet them.

In your communications with your child, advise them that someone from a chat room may want to meet with them personally after establishing an Internet friendship. They should inform you immediately if someone does request such a meeting. Discuss the potential dangers of this type of meeting. If you are familiar with your child's chat room discussions and are comfortable with a meeting taking place, first, have your child inform the Internet contact that you, the parent, will be present at the meeting, and second, insist that the initial meeting be in a public place.

Know your child's chat rooms and cyberspace interests.

A chat room is space where someone in their own private area can "chat" with people from all over the world. These chat rooms are generally tied to one another by special interests or subject matter. Chat rooms are one of the most popular sites for children. Knowledge of your child's chat rooms will inform you of their special interests you may be unaware of. Monitoring these Internet areas will enable you to curtail any potential harmful activity.

Know your child's online friends.

If your child has established regular chat room friends, you should get to know these friends by occasionally joining the chats. This is especially necessary if your child wants to meet the online acquaintance. Remind your child that the person on the other keyboard is still a stranger, and you should feel comfortable with them also. It would be advisable for you to contact the other child's parents prior to allowing a meeting between the children, and remember to go with your child on their first meeting, in a public place.

Advise your child not to call someone from the Internet without your permission.

Predators know that caring parents educate their children with child safety rules such as "do not give your personal information to anyone on the Internet," so the chat room pedophiles give their own telephone number to their "new friend" online and convince the child to call them. When calling the number provided, the unsuspecting child gives the pedophile your telephone number when Caller ID displays it. Make it a regular practice to screen your child's chat room activities, and only when you feel comfortable with extending the level of contact should you give permission for your child to do so.

Teach your child to not open e-mail from an unknown source.

Obscene and pornographic material is often sent with "catchy" subject titles such as "You have got to see this!", "Is this puppy yours?", 'Look at this!", and many other sayings to arouse the curiosity of the best of us, especially children. If your child does not know the source of the e-mail, advise them that opening it may reveal such obscene material or it may harm the computer with a virus. If, unknowingly, the message is opened, this is the type of subject matter that should be reported to the authorities such as the National Center for Missing and Exploited Children (NCMEC).

If your child receives offensive or obscene material on the Internet they should report it to you immediately.

General communications with your child pertaining to offensive or obscene material will instill a sense of comfort in reporting to you these onscreen messages. They should not feel guilt or embarrassment in receiving this material. The NCMEC monitors this type of activity. If such material is received, report it immediately to their Cybertipline at 1-800-843-5678 or www.missingkids.com/cybertip.

Protect a child from harm and

the child will have a safe night.

Teach a child to be safe and

the child will have a safe life.

10

Personal

Teach your child that adults should not have secrets with children.

We have all heard stories about a child being told, "This is our little secret," as an adult or older child molests the young child. Secrets between adults and children are wrong. If an adult tells your child to keep a secret, inform your child that it is okay to tell all secrets to you. It would be wrong to keep a secret from a parent. Explain to your children that secrets involve words, never touching, never anything that makes them feel uncomfortable, and never things that they do not like.

A swimsuit is a guideline to private body areas.

Any part of the body covered by a swimsuit or underwear is your child's private area, not to be touched by anyone (other than a physician or a care provider needing to assist in cleaning your child). If someone touches your child in any private area, tell your child to move away from the person immediately and tell you as soon as possible. Explain to your child that if someone touches any private area, even while playing or tickling, that it is wrong. Teach your young children to say, "Don't do that!" when someone is touching them and they don't like it.

Note that your child has moods, as does everyone. One day he or she may feel comfortable, even excited, in hugging Grandpa, but the next time they may shy away or simply refuse. This does not indicate that Grandpa is a molester or has offended the child, only that your child is not in an affectionate mood on that particular day. Never insist that a child show someone affection such as hugging or kissing. A child's affectionate personality will develop naturally with the love and affection they receive from their parents.

Teach your child about inappropriate touching.

One young sex offender may spend the rest of his life in prison thanks to the testimony of a brave little 5-year-old girl. The pedophile molested the little girl at a day care center and the girl told her parents about the incident. The mother of the victim testified in court that she and her husband had taught their daughter about inappropriate touching.

As stated previously, use every opportunity to discuss sensitive issues with your child, media stories, "what if" scenarios, etc. Discussing sensitive issues with your child is not meant to suggest sitting down in a "teaching" format, but rather a very informal approach. As a situation arises, approach the issue at hand. One opportunity may focus on abduction, the next on a molestation article, and another on other areas of child safety. These are the opportunities to discuss with your child what they would do in exact or similar circumstances.

Have your children tell you immediately if an adult starts showing them an extra amount of attention.

Child molesters in trusted positions generally attempt to "warm-up" to a child they are focusing on as their next victim. If your child says anything to the effect of "Mr. Teacher is acting funny," pay close attention to the messages; they may signal danger. Touching raises an instant flag. Be aware of actions that do not involve other children, such as a short trip to lunch, gifts, or an invitation to a sporting event. While a child's radar may be set to pick up on "Stranger" activity, it might not be attuned to pick up signals from a trusted adult. Many children may feel they are being singled out as a reward for being a good student or for having special talents required for a certain project, thereby justifying the "special treatment." If any favorable treatment is directed to your child, investigate promptly and, if necessary, report it to the proper school or law enforcement officials.

Have your child report anyone who exposes their private body areas.

If anyone exposes himself (or herself) to your child, teach your child to immediately get away from the person and report the incident to a trusted adult. As soon as possible, your child or the adult who received the report should write down a brief description of the offender, where it took place, and the time of the exposure. Predators expose themselves hoping to arouse the curiosity of a child or to stimulate their own sexual gratification in observing the child's reaction. Sex offenders may expose themselves to a child in a public restroom or call the child to a vehicle where they are sitting exposed. Immediate reporting may help apprehend these individuals and deter future incidents.

Your child should report anyone showing inappropriate pictures.

Pornographic pictures are common lures by child molesters to attract new victims. Be aware of your child spending an inordinate amount of time with an adult or an older child, especially if the time is at the other person's home. Pedophiles commonly entice young children to their homes with offerings of video games and refreshments, and invariably soon begin showing the children pornographic pictures or movies. Many molestation victims attest to the fact that they were drawn into the pedophile's trap under such conditions.

If a child is well-versed in child safety education and knows how to react to someone attempting to entice a child into a sexual encounter, another child may not be. Reporting everyone showing inappropriate pictures to children may prevent an innocent child from becoming a child molester's victim.

May your child never be afraid

and always feel safe.

11

Family

Your children should know that you trust them and will believe them.

Children should know that they are loved and trusted so they will feel comfortable discussing anything with their parents. A child will hesitate to discuss sensitive subjects with parents for two main reasons: they feel embarrassed, or they feel they will not be believed, especially if it is their word against that of an adult. When children are sexually molested, they may feel guilt. They will believe others will blame them for the assault. Never let a child feel they are at fault for being a victim of a sexual predator. Let them feel love, compassion, and understanding. Confident children know that they can discuss anything with parents.

Build your child's self-esteem.

A child lacking self-esteem would be susceptible to the compliments and flattery of a stranger, whereas a child whose self-esteem is continually built up will be self-confident.

The self-confident child will be more likely to ward off any advances made by those with ill intentions.

Predators will praise a child and present themselves in every imaginable way to be a person the child can trust, the "nice guy" who makes the child feel special. Criminal sex offenders have stated that they looked for children who seemed sad, the children who seemed they felt the world was against them, the children who felt that nobody cared. These children were poised as easy prey for the child predators. Let your child know they *are* special, continually build their self-esteem and self-confidence.

Let your child know you are always there for them.

Advise your children starting at a very young age, and continually remind them as they become young adults, that they can call you for help any time, for any thing, under any circumstances.

Every child has been or will be in a situation where they feel, "My parents are going to kill me." He or she may have been in a fender-bender with the family car, experimented with alcohol, or foolishly run off with someone, and subsequently regretted his or her actions. This is the time children need parental guidance and assistance. They will need you to be there for them.

Child abductors and sexual predators look for the vulnerable, scared child, and want to be helpful to any child in need, only to spin their web and draw in their prey. Be your child's parent and also their friend. Be the one they know they can always depend on in any circumstance.

Child safety is

the ultimate parental responsibility.

12

Documentation

THIS CHAPTER will assist you in creating a thorough personal child identification folder. In the event your child ever is missing, this information would be extremely helpful to law enforcement agencies or anyone assisting in searching for your child.

Standard procedures are followed by law enforcement officials when a child is reported missing. The information in your self-created folder will expedite an officer's efforts and allow that officer to immediately perform a very thorough search. FBI agents have stated that the most critical times of a search are the first few hours a child has been missing. Initial efforts should cover as much ground as possible. As you glance through and begin recording the recommended information, documenting all areas and activities of your child's life, you will realize practically "no stone will be left unturned" by those looking for your child.

It is recommended that this information be updated on a regular basis, every six months for younger children and annually for an older child, especially updating the photos of your child.

The major content of your child identification folder is documentation, therefore as you record the various information establish a separate log for each section, for example, identification card, residence, school, etc. This information can be recorded and maintained on a computer disk, but for easy access have a printed or written copy readily available.

As you complete your documentation of each area check the space indicating it has been recorded in your folder.

Child Identification Information

- Identification Card
- Child's Full Name and Nicknames
- Address
- City
- State
- Zip Code
- Home Telephone Number
- Emergency Contacts
- Phone Numbers
- Date of Birth
- Sex
- Height
- Weight
- Left or Right Handed
- Hair Color
- Eye Color
- Blood Type
- Race
- Hair Style
- Identification Marks
- Birthmarks
- Scars
- Glasses
- Medical Problems
- Medications
- School Name

- **School Address**
- **School Phone Number**
- **Physician Name**
- **Physician Address**
- **Physician Phone Number**
- **Dentist Name**
- **Dentist Address**
- **Dentist Phone Number**
- **Contact Information**

An officer arriving at the scene of a missing child call will have two preliminary questions in addition to the above information, as he or she prepares to broadcast an initial report that will be picked up by all adjoining police agencies: "Where was the child last seen?" and "What was the child last wearing?"

Every parent in such a situation will naturally be in a "state of shock". The above information will allow the initial broadcast and subsequent search; therefore, be as mentally prepared as possible, under such circumstances, by noting the answers to the above two additional questions.

Fingerprints

Fingerprints are as valuable as DNA as a physical means of identification, that is, without any photos or eyewitnesses; therefore, fingerprints must be clear and identifiable. No two people have the same fingerprint. Each print is distinguished by loops, swirls, and arches, among other identifiable marks.

Due to the importance of the clarity of your child's fingerprints (and for younger children, palm prints) it is recommended that you have a professional take these prints. A fingerprint cannot be sufficiently identified if it smudged or if it is only a partial print. Police agencies may take your child's fingerprints for you as a public service or for a minimal fee, or they may be able to recommend a professional service that will take them for you. Also be aware that there are numerous community activities where free fingerprinting is offered for children. These service providers are generally very competent in the fingerprinting process, as they have most likely been doing these events for many agencies, or are very likely to be police officers assigned to the community service day. Be on the lookout for such events and take advantage of having your child professionally fingerprinted for your child identification folder.

Family Information

Make a complete list of all relatives who have had contact or might have future contact with your child. List names, relationship, addresses, and all known contact numbers on each person.

This is important information that may lead to discovering your child was en route to visit a relative, that a relative has picked up your child, or that someone involved in a custody battle with you has taken the child.

If you are separated or divorced, provide all information pertaining to legal and physical custody, any visitation schedule, and whether there have been any custody problems.

List all information on any individual who has access to your residence, such as household employees, relatives, friends, etc.

Friends

List information on any family friend who frequently visits your home. Especially list the information on any person with whom your child is comfortable.

Provide as much information on your child's friends as possible, all contact numbers, residence addresses, hobbies and interests, etc.

Many children have been located playing with friends, or after spending the night with a friend who had no telephone. Teach your child to always notify you of their intentions and first obtain your permission to be away from home overnight.

Medical and Dental

List your primary physician's name, address, and telephone number.

List all information pertaining to a specialty physician, if applicable.

Provide a list of all medications prescribed for your child. List any allergies your child may have.

When was your child's last medical visit and what was the reason for the visit?

Any major concerns regarding your child's health? Any special needs?

List your dentist's name, address, and telephone number.

When was your child's last dental visit what was the reason for the visit?

Does your child wear braces?

Any major concern regarding your child's dental health?

Medical and dental information is of utmost importance and necessary for anyone assisting in the search for a child. Are there special medicines or treatments that must be pre-pared? Were medications taken? When? How frequently are they required? Any stress-related problems? Medical and dental information is also critical should identification be necessary.

Activities

The purpose of this section is to be able to determine where your child should be within given time frames, who they may be with, and what they may be doing. In the event your child is late coming home or fails to show at a scheduled appointment, this information would effectively narrow the scope of the search.

Keep a detailed list of your child's activities in your child identification packet. *This packet is for home storage only—not to be given to anyone except in an emergency situation.*

Following is a suggested activities outline for your Child Identification Packet:

- School schedule. Include all classes and after-school activities.
- All participation in sports activities.
- General activities, such as ballet, music lessons, hobbies, etc.
- Any employment? Where? When, Hours? Days? Contact person.
- Parental visitations.

List all transportation your child may utilize, such as school or public buses. Note the bus schedules.

Any carpools? With whom do they travel? Be specific.

What are the routes to and from home? List all alternate routes.

Document all locations your child has expressed a special interest in, such as the cabin at the lake, the bowling center or arcade, their friend's home, and other special locations. List as many places as your child has discussed as "one of my favorite places."

Internet

General Internet documentation must include any e-mail addresses and known passwords. Internet activity is a great source for information leading to interests, activities, and associates.

List your child's favorite web sites, any Internet friends, and their favorite chat rooms.

If your child has ever met someone, in person, after meeting on the Internet, give complete details and information on the person they met. Are they still meeting? Acquainted?

Miscellaneous Information

Review all the information you have documented on your child to this point and any information you feel may also be relevant. Store this packet in a secure location where it will be readily available should your child ever become missing. Hopefully you will never need to provide this information to anyone.

Keep a growth chart in your home to track your children's growth and to accurately document their heights every few months during their younger years, as they grow so rapidly.

A Personal Child Identification Folder is recommended for each child.

13

General Child Safety Rules

Home Safety Rules

- Have a residential alarm system installed in your home
- Teach your children the codes to all alarms in your home.
- Children younger than teenage years should not be left home alone.
- Inform your child of emergencies that warrant calling 911.
- Always keep emergency telephone numbers, 911 and family contacts, readily available.
- In case of an emergency your child should know who to call first, and all who should be contacted.
- Make a list of house safety rules regarding visitors, telephone calls, alarms, etc., and review it often.
- Prepare and practice with your children an emergency evacuation plan in your home—review your plan periodically.
- Have a fire extinguisher in your home. Everyone should know how to use it.
- Document all suspicious telephone calls and "hang up" calls.

Neighborhood Safety Rules

- Be a good neighbor, report criminal activity on your block.
- Get involved in a Neighborhood Watch program.
- Report all suspicious vehicle activity in your neighborhood.
- Volunteer your home as a safe home for children.
- Know your neighbors. Watch their homes and have them watch yours.
- Inform your neighbors on how to reach you in an emergency.
- Lights deter crime. Keep your neighborhood well lighted.
- Advertise against criminal activity, use Neighborhood Watch and Child Safety Zone signs.
- Introduce your children to your neighbors so everyone knows where the children live.
- Show adult presence; supervise small children playing in your neighborhood.

Medical Safety Rules

- Know the location of the nearest hospital and after-hours emergency care facility.
- Have information readily available on any allergies your child may have.
- Have readily available a list of medications required by your child.
- Provide emergency medical releases to all babysitters, care providers, and your child's school.
- Maintain a home identification file that includes a copy of your child's medical records.
- Keep an adequate first-aid kit in your home.
- Have a basic knowledge of First Responder Medical Aid and CPR.
- Never hesitate to call 911 for a medical emergency. Time can be a critical factor.
- If your child has a medical condition, he or she must carry information identifying the condition.
- Keep a list of emergency medical centers accessible, such as the Poison Control Center: 1-800-222-1222.

Vehicle Safety Rules

- Never leave small children alone in a vehicle for any reason.
- A safety seat belt should always be fastened when a vehicle is in motion.
- Car doors should be locked and the windows left up, especially when the vehicle is stopped at a corner, light, or off-ramp.
- Control your children's door and windows.
- Never let children play in any area of an unattended vehicle.
- Do not allow children to put any body part out the window of a moving vehicle.
- Have an automobile first aid kit in your vehicle in case of a minor accident.
- Have your child's safety seat properly inspected at an official inspection station.
- Make sure your child's safety seat is the correct seat for the weight of your child.
- Children 12 years and younger should always ride in the back seat, preferably in the middle.

School Safety Rules

- Advise your child about peer pressure and the problems it may cause.
- Tell your child never to do something because of a "dare."
- Bullies should be reported, and the bully's actions should be discussed with the school teachers.
- Make sure your child's school is a weapons-free environment and enforces a "no tolerance" policy.
- Your child's school should contact you immediately if your child is absent or excessively late.
- Insist that the school notifies all parents of any violent activity on the school campus.
- Have your child inform you if there is gang activity at the school.
- Know your child's school security rules and enforcement policies.
- Have regularly scheduled meetings with school officials to discuss potential dangers.
- Encourage your child's school to teach child safety and drug awareness programs.

Drugs and Gun Safety Rules

- Discuss the dangers of drugs with your children. Tell them to let you know immediately if someone offers them drugs.
- A child should always say "No" to anyone offering them any type of drug.
- If your child sees someone with drugs, have them tell a teacher and you.
- Be familiar with the signs and symptoms of someone using drugs.
- Report any known drug activity in your neighborhood or playground areas.
- Explain to your child that guns can be dangerous and are not to be played with.
- Any loaded weapon should be kept in a locked, safe location inaccessible to children.
- Tell your child to report it if they see anyone displaying a gun.
- Always consider a weapon loaded and never point a gun playfully at another person.
- Inform your child to immediately get away from anyone with a gun.

Travel Safety Rules

- A child traveling alone should not carry tickets openly.
- If a child gets lost while traveling, he or she should approach a uniformed employee, e.g. an airline pilot, flight attendant, restaurant worker, etc.
- A child should never wear identifying tags on the outside of his or her clothing, backpacks, or luggage, especially when traveling alone.
- In a hotel, tell your child which floor your room is on, show them where it is, and how to get to the room.
- Children should be familiar with how to make a telephone call from a hotel room.
- Coordinate all details for a child traveling alone: the adults involved, the schedules, and the times to notify everyone involved.
- Discuss with the airline its policies and procedures in accommodating a child in the event of a delayed flight.
- Provide for a child to be escorted if he or she needs to change transportation, airplanes, buses, trains, etc.
- Create your own "Child Safety Zone" within your arm's reach whenever you travel. Keep your guard up!
- Advise your child to keep to their schedule and never allow an unknown person to escort them anywhere.

What If . . . What Would You Do?

THE "WHAT IF" GAME. This is one of the most powerful learning techniques for children, as well as adults in every profession. This practice places children in scenarios where their decisions will teach and re-enforce child safety rules.

Use the following questions as guidelines for incorporating your family method of interaction with your child. Multiple-choice questioning is only one method of presenting hypotheticals. Play the "what if" game for all the child safety rules as the safety topic becomes appropriate, such as when a child safety issue is featured in the media.

What if your mommy was in the shower and you were playing alone in the house when the doorbell rang and a man outside said, "Hello, it's the Ice Cream Man!" What would you do?
  (A) I would open the door and get some ice cream.
  (B) I would open the door and see if it really is the ice cream man.
  (C) I would open the door, tell him mommy is in the shower, but I could see what he had.
  (D) I would say in a loud voice, "My mommy can't come to the door right now, come back later."

(D)

What if you were playing on the swings at the playground and a stranger lady came up to you, said she was very sad, and asked if you would help her find her white kitten, Snowball? What would you do?

- (A) Get off my swing and run away from the lady, and tell someone about her.
- (B) Ask her where the kitten went and look in that area.
- (C) I like kittens so I would go with her and help.
- (D) Help her find Snowball—she was sad.

(A)

What if someone came into your room late at night, picked you up and said "be real quiet and everything will be fine," and if they started carrying you out of your room? What would you do?

- (A) Nothing, because they said everything would be fine if I was quiet.
- (B) I would be quiet because I wouldn't want to wake everyone else.
- (C) Scream as loud as I could and kick hard, because others will wake up and help me.
- (D) I would keep quiet because if I were wrong, I would be embarrassed by screaming and waking everyone.

(C)

What if you wanted to play in the neighborhood but no one else could play with you? What would you do?

    (A)   Go outside and play. We have a safe neighborhood.

    (B)   Go to the other homes to see if someone can come out and play.

    (C)   Go outside and while playing I would watch out for bad people.

    (D)   Stay inside until someone could play with me. I know it's only safe to play with a buddy.

                                    (D)

What if you are in a shopping mall and you lose sight of your mother? What would you do?

    (A)   Stay where I last saw her, and ask someone to help find my mother, but I would not go with anyone anywhere.

    (B)   Go back and wait by our car.

    (C)   Try to find my mother in another store, one that she likes.

    (D)   Walk around the mall until she sees me.

                                      (A)

What if someone said, "You look like a model. I'll give you a hundred dollars for your first photo session if you'll come to my van and let me take your picture." What would you do?

(A)   Ask for the money first and then go only for one picture.

(B)   Get away from the person as fast as I can and report them.

(C)   Ask if others had their pictures taken and then, if so, I guess it would be okay.

(D)   Go with the person and see if it was a real studio in the van.

(B)

What if you are walking home and a car pulls up, slowly drives near you and a stranger calls for you to come over to the car? What would you do?

(A)   Keep walking and ignore the person.

(B)   Stop and see what the person in the car wanted.

(C)   Turn around and run the other way from the car.

(D)   I would talk to them because it would be rude to ignore them.

(C)

What if you are home alone when someone calls on the telephone and they tell you they are doing a telephone survey and would like to ask you some questions? What would you do?

(A) Tell the caller I never give information to anyone on the phone.

(B) Answer just a few short questions.

(C) Tell them I am alone and they would have to call back.

(D) Ask them where they are from and answer their questions if it is a good company.

(A)

What if someone on the Internet wanted to exchange phone numbers and have you call them? What would you do?

(A) Give them my number and wait for them to call me.

(B) Call them before I gave them my number.

(C) Refuse to give any personal information to anyone on the Internet, and I would not call them because they might have Caller ID.

(D) Give them my address so they could write me before we talked on the phone.

(C)

What if, on the way to school, your friends want you to take shortcut through the alley and old construction area? What would you do?

    (A)   Take the shortcut, especially if we were late for school.

    (B)   Tell them I'll take the normal route. I know to avoid dark and unsupervised areas.

    (C)   Check out the shortcut to see if it really is faster.

    (D)   Take the shortcut, but hurry through as fast as possible.

    (B)

What if you were walking home and you felt that someone was following you? What would you do?

    (A)   Wait for awhile to see if the person was just following someone else.

    (B)   Nothing, because it would be embarrassing for everyone if I was wrong.

    (C)   Stop walking and if the person got near me I would ask why they were following me.

    (D)   Run as fast as I could to a public place for help. I would drop everything so I could run faster.

    (D)

What if, after school, your friends did not want to go home but want to go to the mall? What would you do?

    (A)   Go with them because they are my friends.

    (B)   Go to the mall and tell my parents later.

    (C)   Call and ask for my parent's permission, or I would go home if I couldn't reach them.

    (D)   Go to the mall but tell my friends I would be unable to go again without permission.

    (C)

What if someone you know touches you in a bad way, in your private area, and tells you not to say anything because no one would believe you? What would you do?

    (A)   Not tell anyone because everyone would believe the adult, not me.

    (B)   Tell my parents because I know they love me and would believe me.

    (C)   Not say anything because I would be embarrassed.

    (D)   Not tell anyone because they would think it was my fault.

    (B)

What if someone told you that your mother was involved in an accident and that you needed to go with them to the hospital? What would you do?

    (A)   Go with them. I would be in a hurry to see my mother.

    (B)   I would tell them no, and would immediately check with a trusted adult.

    (C)   Go with them if I knew who they were.

    (D)   Only go with them if the hospital was nearby.

    (B)

What if an adult kept hugging and tickling you and you didn't want them to? What would you do?

    (A)   I know I can say no to an adult. I would say, "Stop doing that!"

    (B)   Move away from them and hope they wouldn't do it again.

    (C)   If they were someone I knew, I guess I couldn't do anything.

    (D)   They would probably just be kidding, so I wouldn't say anything.

                                        (A)

What if the school bus was late on a rainy morning and someone said they work for the school and they will give you a ride to the school? What would you do?

    (A)   Ask to see some identification and then take the ride.

    (B)   I know never to take a ride with a stranger or even someone I know without my parent's permission. I would say no and then run home.

    (C)   I would take a ride because it was raining.

    (D)   Since the bus was late and I had to get to school, I would take the ride.

                                        (B)

15

Notable Laws and Alerts

"Code Adam"

"Code Adam" is named for Adam Walsh, a six-year-old boy whose 1981 abduction from a Florida shopping mall and subsequent murder helped raise awareness about child abductions.

If a customer reports his or her child missing within a store, gives a brief description to a store employee, the employee broadcasts a "Code Adam" alerting specially trained employees of the missing child. The employees stop what they are doing and begin searching for the child. The employees monitor all exits and search the store and parking lot. These employees know when to alert the authorities.

"Code Adam" was created in 1994 and has been implemented in more than 36,000 stores nationwide.

"Amber Alert"

"Amber Alert" was created in 1996 in memory of nine-year-old Amber Hagerman. Amber was kidnapped while riding her bicycle in Arlington, Texas and she was subsequently murdered. Local residents began contacting radio stations in the Dallas area suggesting they broadcast special "alerts" to prevent such future incidents.

Since its inception in Dallas, the Amber alert plan has expanded to many states nationwide and has been credited for saving numerous abducted children.

"Megan's Law"

"Megan's Law" is a national law in memory of Megan Nicole Kanka. In 1995, a convicted child molester was arrested for the murder and rape of seven-year-old Megan Kanka in New Jersey. The convicted child molester lived across the street from the Kanka residence and the Kanka family had no knowledge of their neighbor's conviction. The law, at that time, did not allow release of sex offender information to the public. In 1996 "Megan's Law" was signed and the public now has access to this type of information.

Registered sex offender information is available by contacting your local law enforcement agency. Many agencies file this information by zip code. Sex offender information may be available in some areas on your law enforcement's website. This is public information and a reason for the request is not required.

National Missing Children's Day

National Missing Children's Day was first recognized on May 25, 1980 after the disappearance of six-year-old Etan Patz in New York City after being allowed to walk to the bus stop by himself. Etan has not yet been found.

In 1983 President Ronald Reagan proclaimed May 25th as National Missing Children's Day in remembrance of the Nation's missing children. This day reminds everyone not to forget our missing children. In 1984 Canada recognized May 25th as National Missing Children's Day.

Glossary

Abduction, illegally carrying off a person by force or fraud.

Amber Alert, see chapter on Notable Laws and Alerts.

Babysitter, someone looking out for the welfare of a child while the parents are away.

Background Check, investigation of a person's references, employment, and education history, and whether the person has a criminal record.

Bodyguard, a person's escort or personal guard. A person assigned to protect someone from harm.

"Buddy System," children playing together. The safety in numbers concept. Children watching out for each other. A deterrence for the majority of pedophiles who prey on the lone child.

Bully, someone who uses his or her strength or power to hurt or intimidate another person.

Child Abuse, mistreatment of a child by harm or neglect.

Chat Room, an Internet tool that allows real-time chatting between all parties with computer access.

Child Molestation, annoying or pestering a child in a hostile way or in a way that causes injury. This term is commonly referred to as sexual molestation, thereby causing physical or mental injury.

Code of Silence, an unwritten bond or statement that encourages silence to protect peers in investigations of unauthorized actions.

Code Adam, see chapter on Notable Laws and Alerts.

Code Word, a special word or phrase, a password, kept secret between parent and child to frustrate and attempt to avoid abductions.

Convicted Sex Offender, a person who has been convicted by the judicial system of an offense involving sex.

CPR, Cardio Pulmonary Resuscitation. A first-aid treatment to circulate blood and oxygen to vital organs to prevent damage.

Cyberspace, the virtual space created by computer systems.

CyberTipline, a toll-free number to report pornographic messages or material sent on the Internet, 1-800-843-5678.

Danger, something or someone posing an unsafe situation that may result in harm.

Day Care Center, a location where a child's welfare is entrusted to a child care professional for a specified period of time. A professional, organized babysitter service.

Dead Bolt Lock, a recommended safety lock for your home. Recommended features: a 1" throw, sloping cylinder, and a key on both sides (when home, keep a key in the lock for safety reasons).

Executive Protection, personal guard service to the business world. See also "bodyguard."

First Responder Medical Aid, help that is meant to sustain life and reduce pain and minimize the consequences of injury or sudden illness in an emergency until professional help arrives.

Internet, a system of linked computer networks. Its scope is worldwide and continually expanding. Also known as the World Wide Web and the Information Highway.

Internet Service Providers (ISPs), companies that provide Internet accounts and connections to individuals and businesses. Also known as OSPs, Online Service Providers.

Megan's Law, see chapter on Notable Laws and Alerts.

National Missing Children's Day, see chapter on Notable Laws and Alerts.

National Center for Missing and Exploited Children (NCMEC), Established in 1984, the NCMEC is a leading organization for locating and recovering missing children. It raises public awareness about ways to prevent child abduction, molestation and sexual exploitation. Telephone number: 1-800-THE-LOST. Website: www.missingkids.com

Neighborhood, the homes and area within close proximity of your residence. Familiar people and scenes where children generally feel they are in a comfort zone.

Neighborhood Watch, an organization of neighbors established to deter crime in their neighborhood. A proactive group where everyone watches out for each other and their homes.

Online, active internet connections using a computer for research or chat room activity.

Pedophile, an adult who has a sexual desire for children.

Peephole, a small hole in a door allowing a view of someone on the other side of the door.

Personal Protection Specialist, a highly skilled individual in the profession of protecting others. Also known as a bodyguard.

Pervert, one showing perversion of sexual instincts.

Poison Control Center, the American Association of Poison Control Centers (AAPCC), founded in 1958, is a not-for profit nationwide organization of poison centers and others interested in the prevention and treatment of poisoning. 1-800-222-1222.

Predator, one who preys upon others. In this writing, it denotes the perverted adult who seeks children as his or her sexual victims.

Public Information Act, a law that allows access to information in government records. An officer for public information may not ask why you want the records.

Registered Sex Offender, a person who is required by law to register as a convicted sex offender, allowing public access to their information, such as their address. See Megan's Law in the chapter on Notable Laws and Alerts.

Reverse Directory, a directory that shows an address that corresponds with a telephone number or where a telephone number is followed by an address.

Safe Home, a home established by concerned neighbors for children to go to for protection if they are frightened and seek comfort from a good neighbor.

Safety Awareness, education focusing on making people aware of potential dangers they may face and on keeping people (especially children) safe from others intending them harm.

Screen Name, a fictitious name used on the Internet for receiving e-mail or communicating in a chat room.

Self-Esteem, one's sense of self-respect. Having a favorable opinion of one's self. Feeling self-confident and assured of one's self.

Sexual Abuse, mistreatment of one person by another sexually, usually against the victim's will, or in the case of a small child, without understanding of what is happening.

Stranger, an unfamiliar person. See chapter on Strangers.

Stranger Danger, a common phrase used to encompass a warning to children of the dangers an unknown person may pose.

Telephone Survey, a telephone call, usually from an unknown person, where questions are asked regarding opinions of products or news items. Generally the caller will ask many questions requiring personal information.

Telephone Tree, a system of neighbors alerting neighbors of an event or emergency, such as a missing child. One neighbor calls another, the other neighbor calls one or two others, and so on, until everyone has been notified.

Trusted Adult, a person of authority or family friend, neighbor or relative in whose presence a child would feel comfortable. Such a person would be in a position to render a small child assistance.

Uncomfortable, a feeling of uneasiness. Being unsure of conditions or circumstances.

Victim, a person who is injured, physically or mentally, by the actions of another, or by an occurrence.

What-If Games, hypothetical scenarios to determine what a person would do and how they would react under given circumstances. An excellent mental preparation for "in-the-event-of" conditions.

Afterthought

JOHN DONNE wrote "No man is an island" in the 17th Century. It is a very profound statement. At the same time, and somewhat contrary to this insight is that every child *is* an island, surrounded by a dark sea of predators.

Throughout this writing, it has been emphasized that predators focus on the lone child. The child unaware of safety precautions. The child who lacks self-esteem. The vulnerable child. A child who has a world of knowledge and is self-confident is neither vulnerable nor alone. He or she has the full support of every caring adult.

As responsible parents and adults, we have an obligation to our children and to our communities to continually be aware of the predators who have their sights set on our children. We must strive to educate ourselves so we may pass this knowledge on to our children.

I am hopeful that this book will impart sufficient knowledge to assist in this on-going battle against every parent's worst nightmare, every child's fear, and every community's enemy—the child predator.